Persistere

A Brigid Cycle Chapbook

by

Bethany A. Beeler

©2022

ISBN: 979-8824907971
Beautiful Buddha Books

Other works by <u>Bethany A. Beeler</u>

Above the Stars

Sign of Jonah (short stories)

TransQuality: How Trans Experience Affirms the World

Gods of Rome

The Smoking Inn (Vol. 2 in *The Chronicles of Diana Atestesso*)

Yanter

How to NOT Know You're Trans: A Memoir

The Fire Golem (Vol. 1 in *The Chronicles of Diana Atestesso*)

Mirrororrim

Maria (of the angels)

Hang Girl (Vol. 3 in *The Chronicles of Diana Atestesso*) (forthcoming)

L & the League of Short-Order Cooks (forthcoming)

Brighton's Bluff (forthcoming)

The Engine of the Avenging Angels (forthcoming)

Caerdwain (Vol. 4 in *The Chronicles of Diana Atestesso*) (forthcoming)

The Bishop Tripped (forthcoming)

Master of the Universe (forthcoming)

For more information on Bethany's paintings and novels,
visit

http://bethanybeeler.com

Table of Contents

For Otis

who taught me to smith

a better me

Persistere

Unstill Birth

Persistere

The end is always

Here.

To stand through.
To stand with.
To stand. Alive.

To sit in the nettles and the down.
To rise from slumber afresh and fall in bed well-spent.

To pull the smoke in through lips and
Breathe out fire. To
Swim depths not ready to find. To
Win light's dew on face and
Frost on teeth.

Burn, alive to wick.
Spark
Tread the lim to dank mossy night and
Cast shadow.

Grit, grind jaw, chew over, and
Know its savor and rib.

Persist.

Anima Me

Thing unmade makes me,
Itself an I.
Anima mundi,
Anima me
Am I.

I shew from a dry well
Quick with one I do not know,
Congealing me

Slough skin and skewer writhe in
Life, lief, leave it, leave it
Shed sword
Coat
Pride
Fear
Shed
Lamb, lam, lim on
Doorway. Release
Winter in toothed west wind

Grip writhe rave and scorn where I
Began, begun to be
Free, ushering
Wrenched flesh. Hold fast.
Cast floating scree
Decree

Wrongs, years fore or

More.
Bane on bane, winter-stained
Lips, barren hips
Grind years. Dare I

Sleep.

Anima Me

Winter's Child

Bright swells in
Fog. Patch of sunlit
Garden hoarfrost storms.
Green vies with brown air, hair of
Trees bitter lank in wait of
Snow. Lined
Forehead worries this weather to
Lather. The lathe of heaven
Spins not at my request a
Prize of frozen jewel set in
Spring-pregnant nest.

Everlasting
(for Tuck)

They die in plague, poverty, protest.
Greed grapeshots grace.
He dies asleep. No touch or goodbye.
Fuck sunrise everlasting.
Sunrise to have with him, had with him, gone with him.
No grimace, no squint.
Here and now. This moment
Everlasting.

Needed Here

Awake. Your silence

Cold rebuff. I
Talk around where we are we are here. You

Watch my shadow write this lie—
Me, shoulder bent, apron rent, hammer
Sparks no
Flash

Bitter lash, rowing throngs, undinal songs
Piracy on the seize undone in labor. I am

Messenger you hate at sunrise,
Kill at dusk. I

Bear your
Stripes. What solace you
Keep!

Mark this goat. For sins

Not me, till its
Duty
Suits you never. All withheld.

I've to know you.

Words aren't needed here.

Thought Lost

Sun warms morning crystal
Branches stream
Pulse-coffined ice, stones, other bones.
Wind whispers gone and
Gone. Snow-pollen garden
Blossom afterglow.
Burrow children, sleep no
Stir. Light watches
Three drips each. One
Green twig betrays
Rhythm in silence.
Rapt in winter mourning,
Drop of sun warms
Frosted
Tombs of friends thought lost.

Bethany A. Beeler

Covenant

It was in this season that I transformed. An
Elk carcass split in two, its
Ends straddle road.
Snow whittles windshield. The
Medium transmutes the message. Alchemy of

Brigid. I once

Feared late winter,
Cold gnawing bones of what I
Thought I was,
Pierced to core.

Strive to quicken
Cold gripped joints
Frozen recognition

Cut in two.

Through.

Phantasm

Final Storm

Shift and clear rise. Droplets
Fleck windshield and lips. Lightning
Start. Frozen wonder, wide drops
Dream windshield runny, thunderhead
March for final
Storm. Searing slash and report, the
Seeds of poem wound tight in chest of poet
Tossing in cave under hill. Blink.
Sink into valley. Downshift
Roll to exit.

Long highway
Arches desire to thinness,
Driving fill-up to fill-up, indigo at headlights'
Edge. Hedge
Pause spooks

Me. Flick ashes.
Switchgrass hiss at shoulder.
Chase its
Lonely tongue. Colloquy of
None hurls me into seat to
Bed to whispering union of
Pillow to head.

Poet Under Hill

Nothing Pollute

Languid lips
Phantasm plunge.

Nothing will pollute this good sleep
Wind nor rain
Nor landing
Buoy bellwether cast on thousand seas. No

Foot tread
Landing. Hope.
Tick-tock, tick-tock, tick-tock till

Boom.

Tear-misted waste, years
Toil, sunder, rack and roll,
Salt seas
Mount moist sky. A final

Plea,
Something not nothing.
Yield
Desire.

Pretended lips
Mouthing why not,
Why wrought,

What then?

But sad toil
Rip and tear,
Rip and tear. I
Dare a
Grain of sand then
Land.

Crow call comes
Fall of expect, except I wait and
Plait tresses for tower rescue. I
Am under

And one.

This sleep will not pollute.

Summons

For those waiting summons,
Buildings talk
Night.
Silent corridors, behind
Corners and every hall's
Turning, every
Door. "The grave's a quiet
Place. No tone inflection, just
Smokeless silence and low-hung
Notes' dejection."

Faces by Numbers

On the Confidence of a Seraphic Doctor

Angels prod sleep, faces
Moon-crowd.
Flesh-fragrant
Scream light. Walk awake, hail
Meccas. Two
Doors breathe clouded eyes, night road
Measured in light spooks
Flesh.
Round my soul
Beg wide assent to
Burst
Presence,
Grudge companion to
Do without.
Wide, I
Swallow all.
Wings spread leave in hearts they seed—
Flying wide
About, wide out.

In a Mirror Darkly

Had I said moment before I
Picked this razor dream I would see
Father today, I would
Shave like
Listening. Now I
Peer through glass,
See prophet in
Voice. White beard clings to
Scrape
Steam from thought.
Cupped bust
Stare. I
Halt to hear last
Droplet drop, to
Revere this rite that cuts aware to
Father not there.

Bethany A. Beeler

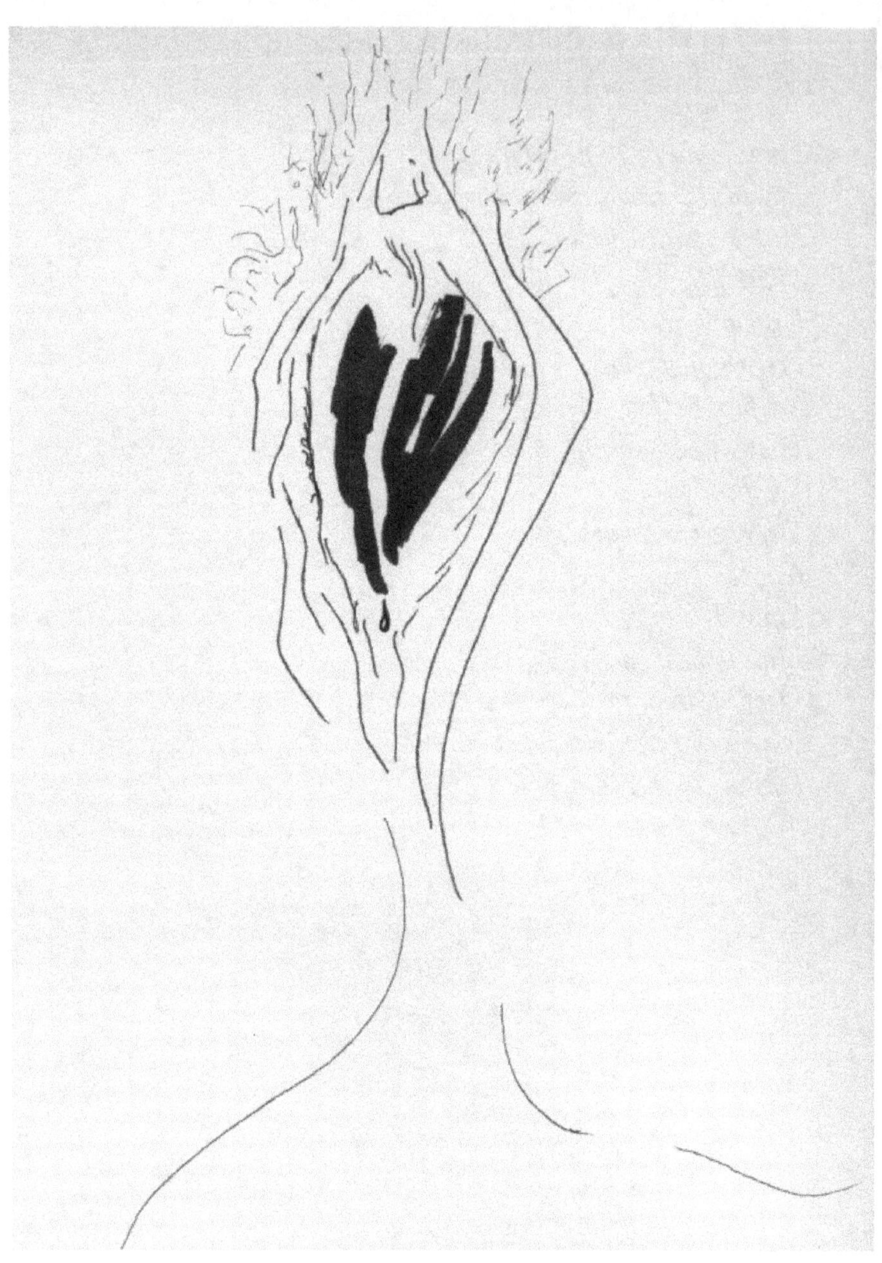

Redolent Dripping

One Night Awoke

Wade this dream
Drift sheets, shadows
Cast in light hem,
Pierced, longing. Let your assent
Trickle lucid
Wounds—

Woken, grope
Tobacco assurance. Ground ash, dim lamp, hand
phosphoresces
sudden in your
Beam. Melt asleep to
Light bleeding trees, the
Salt-fall shudders of a heart on her knees.

Bethany A. Beeler

Abiding

You've philosophies. I've
Tomes of
Teachings ages-old, sold to highest
Bidding,

Biding my time, awash in lime my
Bone. I

Burn this

Ash to last jot and tittle.

Relit, light to
Light
Hearth of
Pocket and
Pouch. Hold
Fire ahand and
Seek morning.

Dry Well

I cup this round
Breast, yeast
Flung in west wind,

Unwound

Voice.

Words aren't heeded here.

You are here.

With

Me, wondering
Snow, afloat a
Berg adrift in
Wield of wight

Winter, weigh eyes,
Choke scent
Thought, ascent. I

Float this sky,
Taste
Sharp sun.

Shield askance, I
Chance glimpse of

Spring in
Grip of frost season,

Sun, a chance of
Flight. I

Play with words, one final
Surd, last
Tongue trem-
or

Hung lip. Grip. Slip.

Let go.

Embrace twists
Guts, sluts of my
Whoring,
Crowd me, hem me. Sin
Tongue finds
Crevasse in dryland empty

Well.

Vision of Otherworld

Drive again,
Vision of otherworld. I
Look from radio talk.
Sunrise transfixes. I'd say

Otherworld's a pleasure dome of
Wish decreed, where fallen
Enemies and cares serve my
God (whom I hold right and Him me) on their knees. Or a

Family-and-friends reunion where all're
Forgiven, I, open-arm
Presiding, indulgent, smiling, not a
Scar where her
Wounds once bled. But I see

Clouded
Sun. Purple fire edges cut me
Through,
False from true. No

Taste the same, fear not fear, no
Pride shame. All plunged in
Bath of
Goddess nursing out my laugh.

Brigid's Day

On Brigid's Day, we'll rise at dawn
And say Matins to the Queen of May,
Put our gold bells and Claddagh rings on
To greet Blessed Brigid's Day.

On Brigid's Day, we'll craft only smiles
On this bonny feast, our labor's play.
We'll laugh like children all the while,
Making none but merry on Brigid's Day.

At Brigid's Noon, we'll say our Mass,
The priest's cloak will be lavender gay.
No dour churchman we'll 'llow to pass
Feast rail on Brigid's Day.

In wane of Brigid's Day, a feast
We'll throw and none will pay
For ale and dancing and pies and sweets.
All's free on good Brigid's Day.

With hush of Brigid's Day, we'll
Rock babes to sleep and say a
Whisper-rosary as we kneel,
Trust our prayers to angels on way to
Heaven gates wide on Brigid's Day.

Otherworld

Hag I Am

Wake to
Empty wells.

Hide us in ditches,
Throng goes by. They
Burn witches, say we lie forbidden
Bed, your hair
Tressed with
Mine. Hand on

Spine grips,
Rips you from grasp. You are not

Mine to
Clasp, chase
Naked on grass while they sing hallows to our end. You are

Me.
I you. We are one and

Being one show lie they
Cast for shroud.

Move about. Hint,
Dare.

Flinch away halted
Nightmare scene they
Cast us in

Rough banks of
Hell-drifted
Snow black and smudge, all
Black and smudge
Till
Light you

Shine on
Dark flank
Scarred by whiplash
Stash against the day they come
Never come, but we
Arriive
Hand-in-hand, no more
Droned on sand in
Deserts we

Make this oasis for to
Drink, hand
Cupped to

Thirst, cursed
No more
We sate each Other.

Grip
Stand
Rapt in vision. Hold

Brush aloft.
Poised,

Poison metal
Taints blood-dream decay. I

Coil, waiting
Witch moment,

Rich foment to
Come from
Hiding, burial shroud striding
Folds, fleet

Ascent,
Dream of what is
Sent in

Message steamed, roiled, coiled, hissing pot boil.
Doubt.

Pause.

Pregnant with.
Float to rim beyond
Scent.

Here.

Phant. Birthe.
Milk leaking my

Dress. Vanity lurch for
Lucre fame, a frame to hang
Myself.

Here I am.
One whole roundness
Cupped in hand.

Coo, cry,
Nurse hoarse throat—
Recognize, damn it! Don't hold me aloft.

Don't warm
Glow.
Shit of living,
Go. It

Cunt
Be this way.

Maze paths
Heart to heart to
Feint of heart to
Drift.

Here.

Wait.

Persist,
Wound, heart-
Shed skin, I am

More than rough-hewn
Moment.

Us. Me.

Here. Now,

Athwart fire licking thighs through loin and
Spread.
Not in head.

Light fire hearth, art to what
Wend?

All iss not dry, she sighs.
  Do i hear

Reply?

Echoes
Skuttle barren ear where no man
Tro'

Holding out Graal. I   am   at last
Here

Cycle my
Gash. Words
Gnash, writhe,
Prophesy

Priestess heady in fume

Plume. Muck blood
Dust, powder shrapnel
Bits of me re-

Assemble, not dissemble these
Feminine rhymes when world afire we play
Marching tune to tomb where
Womb finds stone purchase.
Diamond, melt in my
Fire. In these rings of

Doom, lose
Foot and spread in luxuriant
Bed low coalescing,
Congeal, look to ceiling, wail cry none have heard. At last a

Word.

Rip it out with each push I push to edge. I

Can, you know.

Why say it? To what end that needs to listen but
Me?

Eight is the number of
Infinity
Beast, not slouching to
Grave but I brave beyond.
Imagining won't

Make it so.

Hear me now, you of
Sackcloth ear who silence pangs more myriad than thought,
stout and
Doughty, sword in hand,
Tracking land where others won't
Wrench the prize never

Mine

Explodes me. I orbit thousand stars
Dust and dark matter
Shine no light till
Now.

Here. This

Cycles out my
Grasp.

Leave it. Lief it. Be it. From

Stillness

Comes nothing, darkness,
Silence declares
Word of light. No ear heard. No
Eye seas till shining echo
Angel-brilliant
Tuned being. When I saw and seeing
Listen, I speak and singing
Hasten chorus of word.

Sling song and rude
Dance,
Taste trumpet glare in
Word. Dancing, still Word from
Black song. Bitter,
Sweet dance
Beams
Glance of first final
Word.

Might finally hear
Meaty heart
Pulsing hand,

Bear it? Fuck them! I
Live it. The big

Fuck me

Tied to tree of own planting

Dirt in nails fragrant
Give way to
Birth. I wind every wound,
Find never bound
Here.
Always free.
Let it be.

Let this fuck

Bleed words,

Sounds,
Rounds fired
Roar,
Tear
Every flag, every
Crater,
Every hag
I am.

Arc of Brigid

Always Here

The arc of time nears consummation,
Touches tongue to ear.
No thought casts light,
Shadow shrouds my blaze.
Broken-axle chariot of
Stumble-stunted days. In this season I

Transform.

Stretch-neck,
Slough, grasp it hinge and hasp.

Brigid comes in
Vision-bloody words of light. If I

Believe this all is real, that
It's no cotton mist,
If this is more than what I feel, then
I tremble for its kiss.

We stand in fire, you and I,
Waiting her approach,
Gilded with no ornament, no
Welcome nor reproach.

Trees enfold and bow to us—
Something's present here.
Something holds us back,
Something beyond fear.

At edge of awe we hesitate, flame
Licks our breast,
Dam-burst ventricle
Fuels our flooded quest.

Flotsam, jetsam, life's
Wreck half-lived. Light
Bends doubt on what we give.

"Come to me," she incants. I finally
Meet you here,
Beyond the beard of harries past, I
Clasp you in the err. We

Meet on ground not of earth where slumbers
Rouse our heads. I'll
Clasp the thighs of sodden
Birth, forever leave my dread.

We one once two cut through and through,
Embrace now at the well. I
Stutter-step to finally
Shew a heaven in my hell.

Two eyes look through me, looking
Back no more.
Leave behind all pageantry, the
Whispers and the lore.

I'm nothing but to posture,
Nothing but my ruse.

Nothing that my heart won't foster,
Bitten at the fuse.

Bang the drum slowly, bang it holy, or—
Better yet—danse more true.
Blooming, breaching, bounce beseeching,
Birthing, tick-tock. Boom.

Beyond my walls now
Crashing down in wave from Otherworld,
Brigid of sighs, her jewel I
Prise from grate of mother pearl.

Rote, mote, do the math. This is none of
Plait or sign.
Moons turn three to
Brigid they be
Lamps to shine my path.

I'm real thing worth everything here in hand
Hesilnutte, nettle bush, and every
Grain of sand.

Push out,
Gurgle, breathe. Welcome wave-washed day. With every
Breath, I scream to death it never was this weigh.

Hang
It
On
A
Line not to

Dry, not to
Stiffen the sheets in seed. The
Witch awakes, consort of action to deed.

New morn.

Prosaic? You said it was never
Me. There, I say it, and saying come to
Be.

Three hold hands and stand about the
Fire from cunt that gulfs

Birth, death, final
Breath, a

Thirst unquenched at well. All is
Well in hearth and
Hand and every
Land where whole and sound
Around the fire and dam, awash

An
End.

Coda.
The end was always
Here.

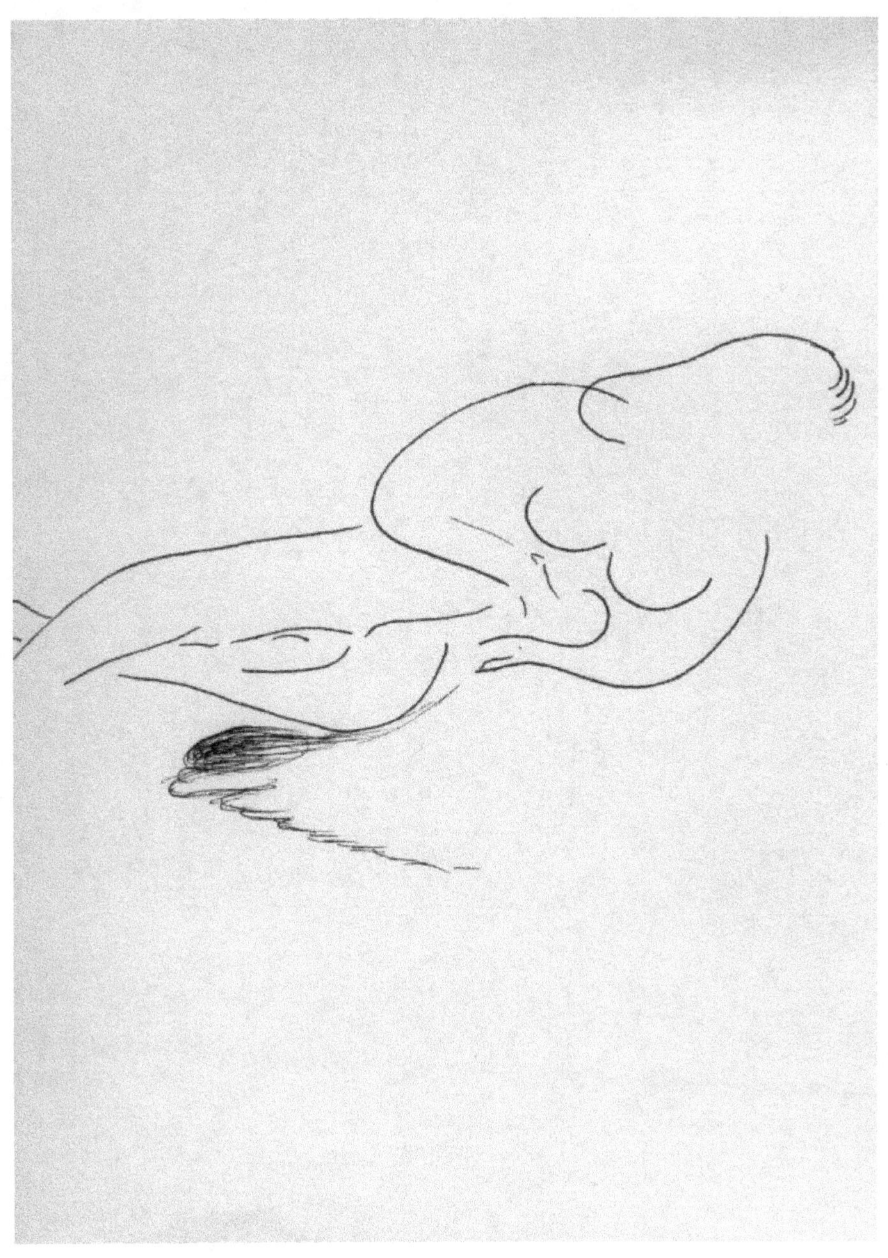

Newborn

Bethany A. Beeler

Wedding Song

You'll remember it was June. I carried
   Lotus and rose, my veil dripped with
   Hyacinth. We drove from Texas this
   Bride and groom. We didn't
   Smile like someone paid for
   Labor but she whose eyes are
   Grace. We came to see
   Children of June birth, this
   Tested love, our golden worth.

Kneeling, we sussed whispered vows to
   Locust songs and raven sounds. Noon
   Sweat-stained glass and
   Twined our silver
   Bands. We smile to each hand-in-
   Hand down aisle. "There's a
   Veil on us," we say to
   Dodge the rice and cries.

Later, we smile moon
   Dancing, me and you, some
   Magic charms our singing
   Gush to whisper doves and trickle
   Wine. We trace our
   Route to fine and private place, not
   Grave or sullen, but blessed bower of
   Laden vines and bee-loud flowers.
   We pause, kiss each a sound, a
   Lip-bound peace our peace has found.

About the Author

Bethany Beeler is a writer and artist who lives in Colorado with her wife, Pamalyn, and three cats of disaster, Big'uns, Frank, and Possum. For more information on her paintings and novels, visit

http://bethanybeeler.com/

Other works by Bethany A. Beeler

Above the Stars

Sign of Jonah (short stories)

TransQuality: How Trans Experience Affirms the World

Gods of Rome

The Smoking Inn (Vol. 2 *in The Chronicles of Diana Atestesso*)

Yanter

How to NOT Know You're Trans: A Memoir

The Fire Golem (Vol. 1 in *The Chronicles of Diana Atestesso*)

Mirrororrim

Maria (of the angels)

Hang Girl (Vol. 3 in *The Chronicles of Diana Atestesso*) (forthcoming)

L & the League of Short-Order Cooks (forthcoming)

Brighton's Bluff (forthcoming)

The Engine of the Avenging Angels (forthcoming)

Caerdwain (Vol. 4 in *The Chronicles of Diana Atestesso*) (forthcoming)

The Bishop Tripped (forthcoming)

Master of the Universe (forthcoming)